COURAGEOUS
CONVERSATIONS

Curated and Edited By: Lisa Fields
Written By: Yana Conner & Sherelle Ducksworth

© 2022 by Jude 3 Project, Inc.

Cover Design: Lance Pettiford
Interior Design: Studio GearBox

All rights reserved. No part of this publication may be reproduced, distributed, or transmitted in any form or by any means, including photocopying, recording, or other electronic or mechanical methods, without the prior written permission of the publisher, except in the case of brief quotations embodied in critical reviews and certain other noncommercial uses permitted by copyright law. For permission requests, write to the publisher at the address below:

Jude 3 Project, Inc.
PO BOX 26206
Jacksonville, FL 32226

Contents

Introduction..4

Chapter One: What is Truth?....................................7

Chapter Two: Can We Trust the Bible?...............17

Chapter Three: Is Jesus the Only Way?.............29

Chapter Four: What is Sin?....................................41

Chapter Five: What is Justice?..............................53

Chapter Six: What Does the Bible Say About Same-Sex Relationships?................................65

INTRODUCTION

In my first year of seminary, I attended the Festival of Young Preachers hosted by the Academy of Preachers. It was a gathering for aspiring preachers and seminarians from various denominational backgrounds.

I was excited to collaborate with my peers and hear the sermons they prepared to deliver at the gathering. In what was called "Preaching Circles," we were intentionally paired with young preachers from different backgrounds and asked to share our perspectives on the sermon delivered that day. The Preaching Circles were particularly formative and foundational experiences that gave birth to the Jude 3 Project's Courageous Conversations conference. The different views shared on the same bible passages were eye-opening and enlightening. I learned firsthand how a person's experiences and education can shape their perspective in a particular way—a way that can be quite different from someone of a different background. My horizon was expanded. I was challenged. I was pushed out of my bubble and into a whole new world. For the first time, I really understood the richness of various perspectives.

Courageous Conversations is our annual gathering that pairs black scholars, pastors, and thought leaders from progressive and conservative spaces to discuss topics relevant to the church and culture. Courageous Conversations has produced rich discussions on various topics. Some of the more popular discussions have shaped the formation of this curriculum. As an organization, we are not just interested in scholars, pastors, and thought leaders having courageous conversations; we want to open the space and equip all Christians to have these conversations as well.

The goal of the *Courageous Conversations* curriculum is to equip you with the tools to effectively have difficult conversations about some of the most pressing issues facing our culture. A courageous conversation is an informed conversation. Therefore, we intentionally explain each argument with the hope of equipping you with the information needed to understand the topic at hand. If you don't understand the argument, you won't be able to intellectually engage it. However, having courageous conversations is not just about being informed, it is also about being compassionate and civil. In a world of hostility, Christians should model compassion and civility in public discourse. We believe that you can contend for the faith without being contentious.

In 1 Peter 3:15, Peter instructs us to be able to give an *apología* or *a defense* for the faith if asked about the hope that we have. However, he doesn't leave it there, he also says that it must be given with *gentleness and respect*. That is our blueprint as an apologetics organization. We have strong convictions and we want to live in a way that provokes questions. When those questions arise, we want to be able to articulate our reasoning with gentleness and respect. That, my friends, is a courageous conversation.

This six-week curriculum will equip you to engage the conversations in culture around truth, the reliability of the Bible, the exclusivity of Jesus, the nature of sin, justice, and sexuality from a black Christian perspective. Jude 3 Project is unapologetically focused on equipping black Christians in apologetics and engaging black culture. That's what makes our organization distinct. There are several apologetics organizations that address these questions but they don't do it through the eyes of color. Jude 3 Project is apologetics from the margins. It is only fitting that this curriculum is written by two people who represent one of the most marginalized groups in the world, black women. Yana Jenay Conner (MDiv) and Sherelle Ducksworth (Ph.D. candidate) are apologists and theologians that bring a rich and fresh perspective to these cultural topics.

I pray that this curriculum equips you to engage in conversations in culture with courage, comprehension, compassion, and civility. As always, I pray that through this curriculum you better know what you believe and why you believe it.

Lisa Fields, Founder and CEO
Jude 3 Project

CHAPTER ONE: WHAT IS TRUTH?

Written By Yana Jenay Conner

Do you know the best way to settle a debate?

Google. Google always knows.

You can always trust Google to tell you the name of that actress in that "fill in the blank" movie. To objectively show you MJ's and LBJ's stats to (once and for all) determine who is the greatest of all time. Or when debating whether the correct term is "coming down the pipe" or "coming down the pike."

Do you know which one it is?

That last debate actually happened. Without an ounce of doubt, I argued with a friend up and down that the expression is "coming down the pipe," not "coming down the pike" and let her know she was wrong. However after we consulted the almighty knower, Google, I was proven wrong. The expression is "coming down the pike."

But to be honest, I still think I'm right. I know what Google says, but my experience tells me differently. I've never heard anyone say "coming down the pike." My friend polled her Instagram community, with the majority affirming that the expression was indeed "coming down the pipe." So I reject the objective origins of this idiom and deem my subjective lived experience as superior. It's my truth!

This is a trivial example of rejecting an objective truth in exchange for a truth rooted in lived experiences, but it's a norma-

At the end of the lesson, you'll be able to answer the following questions:

1. What is the difference between relativism and absolutism?

2. How did earlier philosophers define truth?

3. What historical events led to switching from absolutism to relativism?

4. Does human consciousness and the call for justice create an argument for absolutism? Why or why not?

5. What are some of the primary reasons people, particularly African-Americans, reject the absolute truths of Christianity?

Glossary (In Order of Appearance)

- **Relativism**: A worldview in which a person or clan can decide what's true for themselves without regard for objective facts.

- **Worldview**: A way of thinking that governs how a person or people group live in and interpret the world.

- **Absolutism**: A worldview in which there is a predetermined universal law embedded in all creation, including humanity.

- **Philosophy**: The study of knowledge, reality, and truth.

- **The Art of Living**: The philosophical idea that there is a "science" to life or a particular way to live in order for humanity to flourish.

- **The Enlightenment** (17th-18th century): The age of reason in which absolute truth was questioned, faith was scrutinized, and skepticism towards the Church grew greatly.

tive practice called *relativism* in which a person or clan decides what's true for themselves without regard for objective facts.[1] For example, in this *worldview*, a person or clan can decide for themselves the color of the sky is not blue, what "truths" constitute a crime, and whether or not sex outside of marriage is sinful.

On the other hand, the opposite of relativism is *absolutism* which presumes there is a moral standard embedded into the earth. Meaning that the definition of what is right and what is wrong is predetermined and universal.

With these two theories in mind, in this chapter we'll consider the following questions: (1) What is truth? (2) How do we discern it? (3) Can we determine truth for ourselves or is it predetermined?

---

1. Washington, Brandon. "Philosophy and Worldviews." In *Urban Apologetics*, edited by Eric Mason, 189-203. Grand Rapids, MI: Zondervan Reflective, 2021.

👀 A LOOK AT THE PAST

Questions regarding truth and its origins are typically discussed in the discipline of Philosophy. Early philosophers pursued the idea of truth out of a desire to discover whether or not there was a distinct "art of living" or way of life.[2] However, the early philosophers' pursuit was not merely an intellectual one, but an ethical one. In response to the injustice and immorality surrounding them, they began to consider whether or not there was a universal law or rationale for living in a particular way—a way that would bring about justice, harmony, and human flourishing.

It's important to note that centuries prior to the advent of Christ, these questions gripped the minds of philosophers such as Pythagoras, Heraclitus, and Xenophanes. At the time, each of these philosophers were convinced there was a universal law that existed to set forth a way to live. In their view, if a universal law did not exist and morality could change from human to human, then it was unreasonable to aspire to things such as justice and harmony. However, humans seemed to naturally long for a just and harmonious society. Black scholar J. Deotis Roberts, summarizing Heraclitus' thoughts writes,

> **[Heraclitus]** relates harmony and reason. According to Heraclitus, the cosmos process is governed by law. There is a pre-established principle of harmony in the universe, indifferent to human or divine wills.[3] The order of those things is the work of Fate and Justice...In the midst of all change and contradiction, the only thing that persists or remains the same is the inexorable law that underlies all movement, change and opposition; it is the reason in things, the *logos*.[4]

After his advent, death, and resurrection, the Apostle John proclaims Jesus Christ to be the *logos* Heraclitus spoke of (John

---

2. Roberts, J. Deotis Roberts, *A Philosophical Introduction to Theology* (Philadelphia, PA: Trinity Press International, 1991), 13.
3. Heraclitus is writing in a pagan pluralistic society that believes in the existence of multiple gods, which is his reason for not capitalizing "divine." Here he refutes the different worldviews attached to those gods and asserts there is a Divine pre-established principle of harmony in the universe that surpasses the principles those gods prescribe.
4. Roberts, 24.

1:1).[5] For Heraclitus, truth is a universal law that can be derived from the cosmos (nature). In John 1:1, the Apostle John repurposes Heraclitus' idea as an evangelistic strategy to reveal that the universal law—the "art of living"—resides in the person who created the cosmos, Jesus Christ.

Centuries later, writer and public theologian C.S. Lewis argued for a return to absolutism based on human's shared ideas about what's right and wrong. He writes, "...human beings, all over the earth, have this curious idea that they ought to behave in a certain way, and cannot really get rid of it."[6]

Lewis' "curious idea" of some form of shared human consciousness, has led to ideas such as affordable healthcare for all, the rise of the Black Lives Matter movement, the championing of equal pay for women, and even the idea of tolerance in a pluralistic society. Each of these points of advocacy is rooted in the idea that there is an "art" or "way" in which humans are to live with one another based on the universal understanding that all people are created equal. Without this universal law there is no justification for calls for justice and equality.

Since this is true, some thoughtful questions for us to consider are: Where does the opposition to a universal law come from? When did absolute truth "stop being a thing?" Ironically, when answering these questions, we discover that those who reject absolute truth share the same motivations as early philosophers who were looking for it. They, too, are in search of a more just, equitable, and harmonious society. However, they reject absolute truth because of the ways people have distorted truth and used it to dehumanize and harm others.

For example, many historians attribute the rise of skepticism to "religious wars" during the 11th to 13th century. During this time, Christians persecuted and killed one another over their different beliefs on baptism, communion, and whether or not the Bible should only be written and read in Latin.[7] In addition to these

---

5. The greek word "logos" is translated as "The Word" in our english translations of the Bible. .
6. Lewis, C.S., *Mere Christianity*, (New York, NY: HarperCollins Publishers, 1952).
7 Olsen, Roger E., *The Story of Christian Theology: Twenty Centuries of Tradition and Reform* (Downers, IL: IVP Academic, 1999), 452.

religious wars, known as the Crusades, Christians in the Latin Church initiated wars against Muslims for control over religious sites, such as the Holy Land.

Dr. Roger E. Olson argues these instances of "Christians behaving badly" lead to the questioning of the Enlightenment, which he summarizes as:

1. An emphasis on the power of "reason" to discover the truth about humanity and the world.

2. Skepticism toward venerable institutions and traditions of the past.

3. Emergence of a scientific way of thinking that offered intellectuals an alternative approach to the knowledge that dominated medieval thought.[8]

The knowledge that "dominated medieval thought" are the absolute truth claims of Christianity and other religions, such as Judaism and Islam. The skepticism towards venerable institutions during the Enlightenment was primarily toward the Church.

REFLECTION QUESTIONS:

What's one example of "Christian's behaving badly" that has caused you or those close to you to reject absolute truths?

_____

_____

_____

In light of this section, what are some examples of good reasons to believe in the existence of absolute truth (a universal law)?

_____

_____

_____

_____

---

8. Ibid., 522.

HOW DOES THE BIBLE DEFINE TRUTH?

The Bible affirms the existence of absolute truth and reveals to us where it is found. In the Creation narrative, we encounter a God who not only creates the material world but imprints within it a law—the "art of living." This law is immediately observed in the Genesis 1-2 creation account where God orders creation by separating darkness from light, calling the darkness "night," and the light "day." In the days that follow, God then organizes the waters above and below, speaks dry land into existence, and puts a law into every seed-bearing plant and fruit tree. He proclaims, "Let the earth produce vegetation: seed-bearing plants and fruit trees on the earth bearing fruit with seed in it according to their kinds" (Gen. 1:11). Here we observe God not only creating the material of the seed-bearing plants and fruit trees, but also embedding within the seed-bearing plants and fruit trees a universal law—the "art for living."

On the fourth day the pattern continues, God gives purpose to the lights of the sky declaring them to rule over the day and the night and serve as signs for the days, seasons, and years. On days five and six, God creates the creatures that will reside in the air, water, and land and designs each of them to multiply according to their kind. If God's pattern throughout the creation narrative is to create and then set forth an "art for living" for each part of His creation, why would He divert from that pattern when He reached the creation of humans? Why would He leave his most precious creation to fend for an "art of living" by themselves?

Now, some might respond to these questions saying, "Well, that's what makes humans different from all of creation, right? We have free will, meaning we have the freedom to choose our own "art of living." To this, I would respond, "Yes, but free will doesn't undermine the reality that humans were created to live in a particular way." There is the "art of living" God put before us and then there are the various ways we can choose to develop our own "art of living." Our free will doesn't negate the existence of a predetermined universal law set forth by God. It is for this reason that God puts before us His commands. His commands aren't burdensome-party-poopers (1 John 5:3-4). His commands are the way to life. His commands are the "art of living."

Additionally, in John 14:6, Jesus makes the most audacious claim a person can make about themselves. After Jesus shared with His disciples that He was returning to his Father, Phillip was desperate to know the GPS directions to where Jesus was headed. He asked, "...How can we know the way? (John 14:5)" Jesus responded, "I am the way, the truth, and the life (John 14:6)." In describing himself, Jesus claims to be the embodiment of the way or "art of living," ultimate reality, and the source of all life. Though people are free to choose their own "art of living," it's only the "art of living" found in Christ that is true and brings about life.

REFLECTION QUESTIONS:

What other passages in Scripture speak to the existence of absolute truth?

_____
_____
_____
_____

In today's society, why do you think Jesus' claim to be "the way, the truth, and the life" is controversial?

_____
_____
_____
_____

THE DISTORTION AND MISUSE OF TRUTH IN AFRICAN-AMERICAN HISTORY

During the height of the Civil Rights Movement in 1965, Elijah Muhammed, the founder of the Nation of Islam, wrote emphatically in his book, *A Message to the Black Man*, "There is no hope for the Black man in Christianity."[9] Though it would be easy to blame Muhammed for planting seeds of anti-Christian-

---
9. Elijah Muhammad, *Message to the Blackman in America* (Phoenix, AZ: Secretarius MEMPS Publications, 1973), 220.

> **It is a "miracle of God" that enslaved Black people were still about to discern and "understand the truth of who God was."**
>
> **Dr. Tiffany Gill** Associate Professor of History, Rutgers University

ity in the hearts of African-Americans, Muhammed was merely putting words to the sentiments of many within the African-American community. Christianity and the Bible had been so deeply distorted by professing Christians who endorsed American slavery, white supremacy, and racism. Dr. Tiffany Gill explains, it is a "miracle of God" that enslaved Black people were still able to discern and "understand the truth of who God was."[10] What a miracle indeed! God, even amid such violence and hatred, caused his character to shine through. He captured the hearts of those who had been oppressed by those who claimed to know and love God.

However, many stand in opposition to Christianity and its absolute truths because of how professing Christians historically have distorted truth to oppress and marginalize others. For example, professing white Christians justified the enslavement of Black people based on two false teachings they claimed were taught in the Bible:

- Christianity and slavery are compatible based on Paul's teachings for slaves to obey their masters.[11]
- Noah's curse against Ham led to God creating a racial hierarchy in which Europeans are divinely exceptional and better than their nonwhite counterparts.[12]

Although these false teachings have been widely rejected across Christian denominations in the present, their damage remains. This history has created ethical concerns that require Christians to provide a defense for Christianity and it's absolute truths.

---

10. The Jude 3 Project, "Black History as an Apologetic," July 17, 2018, video, 34:10, https://www.youtube.com/watch?v=XQXTKHM_hJA.
11. Hart, G.I. Hart, *Who Will Be A Witness: Igniting Activism for God's Justice, Love, and Deliverance* (Harrisonburg, VA: Herald Press, 2020), 127.
12. Ibid., 129.

WHAT DOES THIS MEAN FOR APOLOGETICS?

As apologists, our goal isn't to win an argument, but to win a brother or sister in Christ. However, we can't do this without understanding their reason for rejecting Christianity or, in this case, absolute truth. We must also know what and why we believe what we believe. Here are three recommendations on how to engage in relationships with those who struggle to accept absolute truth.

Find Common Ground

In most cases, we can find common ground with a person struggling to accept absolute truth. For example, many people are rightfully angered that those who professed to be Christians distorted Biblical truths in order to enslave Native Americans, Africans, Asians, and other people of color for their own financial gain. This should anger us as well. However, to take issue with how people distorted the truth doesn't mean that we have to throw the truth out with the bath water. No, we just need to throw out the distortion. The truth of the Bible in and of itself is still very good. We can find common ground with their grievances and still provide a reasonable defense as to why we believe in the absolute truths of the Bible.

> "Move towards others with empathy, compassion, and understanding."

Choose Empathy

As previously stated, many people's greatest barrier to accepting absolute truth is the fact that professing Christians have distorted or used truth to exploit and harm others. Their rejection is understandable, especially if they experienced the exploitation or harm first hand. In an instance like this, you have an opportunity to move towards them with empathy, compassion, and understanding. Instead of impatiently walking away or type casting them as militant or stubborn, move towards them. Ask questions, agree when you can, and be lovingly honest when you can't.

Know What You Believe and Why You Believe It

In order to engage in a winsome conversation about absolute truth, you'll need to know what you believe and why you believe it. In this chapter, you were presented with multiple ways to advocate for the reality of absolute truth. We argued for the evidence of absolute truth in creation, the human consciousness, and our shared desire for a just and equitable society. Use these insights and make it a practice to spend time in God's Word, multiplying your understanding of what you believe and why. As apologists, our textbook is the Bible.

REFLECTION QUESTIONS:

What makes you most nervous about defending the reasonableness of absolute truth?

_____

_____

_____

In what ways can you empathize with those who struggle to accept absolute truth?

_____

_____

_____

What are some other common sense ways you can help others see the reasonableness of absolute truth?

_____

_____

_____

CHAPTER TWO:
CAN WE TRUST THE BIBLE?

Written By Sherrelle Ducksworth

Since the Transatlantic Slave Trade, Black people have been subjected to oppressive and dehumanizing authority figures. From forced submission to slave owners, racist Church clergy, Jim Crow laws, and submission to racist and biased law enforcement, our collective experience with authority has included a lot of wickedness. Too often, these oppressive authority figures used the Bible to validate and legitimize their treatment of Black people.

However, even though the Bible was a tool used to legitimize oppressive authority, in the Scriptures, Black Christians found a God who was anti-oppression. In Scripture, they encountered a God who revealed himself as a servant leader whose Word called for the liberation of their bodies and the salvation of their souls.

Historically, the majority of African-Americans have consistently believed the Bible to be the *infallible* and *trustworthy* Word of God and the foundation for life and godliness. However, today, many African-Americans and Black Christians have expressed concerns about the validity and trustworthiness of the Bible. There are three primary contemporary questions regarding the authority of Scripture: **(1)** Has God spoken in the scriptures? **(2)** Are biblical texts without error? **(3)** Is the Bible truthful? **(4)** Does Scripture contain the Word of God or is it the Word of God?

In theology, these questions are discussed under the topics of *special revelation, inspiration* and *inerrancy.* Special revelation deals with the question, *"Has God revealed Himself in the scriptures?"* Inspiration deals with the question, *"Has God spoken through the writers of the Bible and are all their words His words?"* Lastly, inerrancy deals with the question, *"Is the Bible free from error?"*

At first glance, these questions might warrant an immediate yes, yes and yes. However, let's be honest, we all might feel the desire to switch to an *"I'm not sure"* once we get to a passage about slavery or the treatment of women. So, how does the Bible answer these questions?

In this chapter, we'll explore the different views on the authority of Scripture throughout history. Then, we will discuss what the Bible teaches about the authority of Scripture and determine the best way to defend it's authority and relevance for life.

At the end of the lesson, you'll be able to answer the following questions:

1. What are the three major ideas associated with the authority of Scripture?

2. What is special revelation, divine inspiration, and inerrancy?

3. What have African-American Christians historically believed about the authority of Scripture?

4. What does the Bible teach about the authority of Scripture?

5. What are some of African-American Christians' historical social concerns about the Bible?

Glossary (In Order of Appearance)

- **Inerrant:** having no error.
- **Infallible:** incapable of possessing error.
- **Trustworthy:** reliable and dependable as the source of God's truth and special revelation.
- **Authoritative:** possessing supreme authority on all matters of life, truth, and reality.
- **Special Revelation:** The act of God revealing Himself in the Holy Scriptures.
- **General Revelation:** The act of God revealing Himself in creation or nature.
- **Inspiration:** God's enablement of the human writers to record the scriptures without error and fallibility.

👀 A LOOK AT THE PAST

The Bible has always been a vital resource in the African-American Christian tradition. Historically, the majority of African-American Christians have affirmed the trustworthiness of the Bible recognizing the Bible as God's sufficient and authoritative self-revelation. Here is a brief look at what African-American Christians from the mid-1700's to present day have believed about the Bible:

> "The Bible has always been a vital resource in the African-American Christian tradition."

- In 1787, Jupiter Hammon, a poet and preacher, referred to the Bible as the "revelation of the mind and will of God" in which "everything in it is true."[13]
- Charles Octavias Boothe, who began preaching after 1860, called the Bible a sacred book that revealed God to man and "our only and all-sufficient rule of faith and practice."[14]
- E.M. Brawley, a Baptist preacher in the Carolinas, stated in the 1890 book titled *Negro Baptist Pulpit*, that "God's book in its entirety, with the doctrine of plenary inspiration, must be contended for...the Bible is a completed and sufficient book..."[15]
- In that same book, Rufus L. Perry, a baptist minister from Brooklyn, affirmed the inspiration of the Bible and the supreme authority of Scripture.[16]

These affirmations continued through the 1900's and 2000's.

- In a sermon titled *Christ the Center of History,* Caesar A.W. Clark, a pastor and preacher whose ministry began in 1933

---

13. Jupiter Hammon, "An Address to the Negroes in the State of New-York" (1787) Paul Royster, ed., 14-16.
14. Charles Octavias Boothe. *Plain Theology for Plain People* (Washington: Lexham Press, 2017),
15. E.M. Brawley, ed., *The Negro Baptist Pulpit: A Collection of Sermons and Papers on Baptist Doctrine and Missionary and Educational Work* (Philadelphia: American Baptist Publication Society, 1890), 18.
16. Ibid.,36.

and lasted through the late 1990's, identified the Bible as "Word Revelation" originating from the Holy Spirit.[17]

- In her 2015 book, *An Introduction to Womanist Biblical Interpretation,* Nyasha Junior references Womanist theologian Clarice Martin's conclusion that the authority of the Bible is one of the three elements of womanist biblical interpretation.[18]
- In his book *Black and Reformed,* Anthony J. Carter identifies the Bible as divinely inspired, inerrant, infallible special revelation of God and the foundation of any sound theology.[19]
- In his recent publication, *Reading While Black,* Dr. Esau McCalley alludes to the Bible's authority claiming the Word of God to have the final word.[20]

Though many affirm the authority of scripture, some contemporary Christians have challenged the notion that Scripture is authoritative, inspired, and inerrant. These preachers and scholars do not discount the Bible's usefulness, value, or significance as a source for the Christian faith. As a matter of fact, they love the scriptures, but note significant problems they have with biblical text. For example, James Cone, one of the fathers of Black Liberation theology stated, "It is true that the Bible is not the revelation of God; only Jesus is. But it is an indispensable witness to God's revelation and is thus a primary source for Christian thinking about God.[21] To Cone, "God was not the author of the Bible..."[22]

Additionally, many womanist theologians do not presuppose the Bible's authority because of its cultural limitations and problematic texts in which women are made less than or abused.

Others reject rigid notions of inerrancy and believe there are errors in the Bible.

- Womanist scholar Renita Weems asserts that accepting the Bible as inerrant should not be a presupposition to engaging

---

17. Walter B. Hoard, ed., *Outstanding Black Sermons: Volume 2* (Valley Forge: Judson Valley Press, 1979), 26.
18. Nyasha Junior, *An introduction to Womanist Biblical Interpretation* (Louisville: Westminster John Knox Press, 2015), 104.
19. Anthony Carter, *Black and Reformed: Seeing God's Sovereignty in the African American Christian Experience*, 2nd ed. (New Jersey: P & R Publishing, 2016), 29.
20. Esau McCaulley, *Reading While Black: African American Biblical Interpretation as an Exercise of Hope* (Downers Grove: Intervarsity Press, 2020), 20.
21. James Cone, *A Black Theology of Liberation* (New York: Orbis Books, 2010), 32.
22. Ibid., 33.

the Bible.[23]
- Reverend James A. Forbes agrees, stating, commitment to the Bible should include a non-rigid view of inerrancy and a belief in the expansion of truth beyond the scriptural text.[24]
- Womanist scholar and theologian Jaqueline Grant also proposes "contradictions do exist in the Bible".[25]

While African-Americans engage the Bible as a significant text, some accept its full authority, inspiration, and inerrancy. Others approach the text with suspicion and believe it to be flawed. This is where the dividing lines exist among African-American Christians today.

REFLECTION QUESTIONS:

What have African-American Christians historically believed about the authority of Scripture?

___

Why do some African-Americans (Christian and non-Christian) reject the authority of Scripture?the life" is controversial?

___

WHAT DOES SCRIPTURE SAY ABOUT ITSELF?

When it comes to recipes, I'm a skeptic. I will look up a recipe, skim the ingredient list, decide which ingredients I really need, and end up scratching off half the list. In my opinion, recipes "do too much." So when I decide to use a recipe, I only use a

---

23 Katie G. Cannon, Emile Townes, Angela D. Sims, eds., *A Womanist Ethics: A Reader* (Louisville: Westminster John Knox Press, 2011), 56.
24 James A. Forbes Jr., *Whose Gospel? A Concise Guide to Progressive Protestantism* (New York: New York Press, 2010), 6, 25-29.
25 Jacquelym Grant, *White Women's Christ and Black Women's Jesus: Feminist Christology and Womanist Response* (Atlanta: Scholars Press, 1989),100.

third of the ingredients. I'll begin following the directions, but eventually, I start to follow my own path, making tweaks here and there to simplify the process. When the food is ready, I fix my mouth to taste what I believe will taste like one of Patti Labelle's home-cooked meals, but to my surprise, it's terrible. Immediately, I discredit the recipe and accuse the creator of culinary fraud. Then I realize that I have misused the recipe and created something the author never intended. The recipe is not untrustworthy - my approach tainted the result.

Similar to my skepticism toward recipes, many approach the Bible as skeptics because of others' misuse. But we must not deny the Bible's trustworthiness because of those who have taken parts of the text and cooked up their own abusive and oppressive path. Here are three things the Bible says about itself that affirm its trustworthiness.

First: the Bible is God's self-revelation through humans and His Son.

In Genesis, God reveals himself as the Creator and gives His commands to Adam. Subsequently, God continues to reveal himself to humanity and uses humans to speak for Him. Here are some examples:

- Moses spoke to Pharaoh on God's behalf (Exodus 5:1) and received the Law from God to give to Israel (Exodus 19-20).
- The Old Testament prophets heard from God and spoke on His behalf to Israel and their enemies (Isaiah 40; Jonah 3:1-2; Amos 7:15; and Obadiah 1:1). They often used the phrase *"thus says the Lord"* to indicate that they spoke on behalf of God (Joshua 24:2; Jeremiah 33:2; Ezekiel 24:3; and Malachi 1:4).
- Peter confirmed that God spoke through men in the Old Testament (Acts 1:16).
- Paul refers to his commands as coming from the Lord and not from himself (1 Corinthians 14:37).

Jesus' incarnation is the revelation of God. Take a look at the evidence below:

- John the Baptist refers to Jesus as the Word of God that became flesh (John 1:1 and 14).
- The writers of Hebrews and Colossians refer to Christ as the

exact revelation of God (Colossians 1:15 and Hebrews 1:3).

Second: Jesus and the Apostles authenticate the Old Testament as authoritative Scripture

Jesus gives credibility to the Old Testament revelation by referencing the Old Testament in his life and teaching. For example:
- In Matthew 4, Jesus utilizes passages from Deuteronomy 8:3, 6:16, and 6:13 to reject Satan's temptations.
- Jesus referenced David's eating of the showbread in 1 Samuel 21:6, demonstrating his belief in the Old Testament revelation.
- The writer Luke also attests to Jesus reading the words of the prophet Isaiah while teaching in the synagogue (Luke 4:17) and using the Old Testament when teaching on the Emmaus road (Luke 24).

Like Jesus, the early Church and the Apostles used the Old Testament in their learning and teaching, but they also utilized Jesus's teaching. Here are some examples:
- Paul references David from Psalms 14:1 in Romans 3:10-12.
- Peter continues the teaching of Jesus in Acts 2 and quotes Leviticus 11:44 in 1 Peter 1:16.
- The Apostle John recounts the murder of Abel by his brother Cain in 1 John 3.

Third: The Apostles and Early Church authenticated the New Testament as authoritative Scripture

There are scriptures that affirm God as the author of the written word. Take a look at the verses below:
- Paul declared his teachings and ministry as inspired by the Holy Spirit in 1 Corinthians 2:13.
- Paul reiterated the inspiration of the word in 2 Timothy 3:16-17, the most noted passage to affirm the divine inspiration of the Bible.
- Peter affirmed the inspiration of the scriptures in 2 Peter 1:19-21 claiming that "men spoke from God as they were carried along by the Holy Spirit."
- Peter affirmed and recognized Paul's writings as Scripture (2 Peter 3:15-16).

- The New Testament was recognized as Scripture through a rigorous process of canonization in which a text had to meet the following requirements to be recognized as Scripture: (1) Written by or closely tied to an apostle (i.e. Peter, Paul, John, etc.); (2) Widely accepted by the church; (3) Not stand in contradict to any other text recognized as Scripture.

The entirety of the Bible affirms God's special revelation, the Bible's authority, and the inspiration of the written word of God. Thus, we there are viable reasons to trust the Bible as the authoritative Word of God.

REFLECTION QUESTIONS:

How does Jesus' use of the Old Testament affirm that its contents are the Word of God?

_____

_____

_____

_____

AFRICAN-AMERICAN CHALLENGES TO THE AUTHORITY OF SCRIPTURE

The Bible has been used to create and perpetuate unjust systems, and for many people this fact discourages them from of affirming the authority of the Bible. For example, White American Christians and non-Christians used Bible passages such as Genesis 9:24, Colossians 3:22, and Philemon 1:11-14 to endorse and legitzmize chattel slavery. Particularly for African-American women, the use of the Bible to support racism, classim, and sexism creates a unique intersectional experience of oppression and marginalization. Some passages appear to command and support patriarchy and sexism as well as teach and validate slavery. As a result, many reject the Bible as authoritative.

So, how do we reconcile these seemingly problematic and oppressive passages with the idea that the Bible is trustworthy? New Testament scholar Esau McCaulley provides an interpretive tool for difficult passages. McCaulley highlights Jesus' exegetical reasoning of creational intent as an interpretive guide. McCaulley asserts, "when we look at the passages in the Old Testament we have to ask ourselves about their purpose. Do they present a picture of what God wanted us to be or do they seek to limit the damage arising from a broken world."[26] Christ uses similar logic when asked about divorce. In Matthew 19:8 he explains that Moses allowed divorce because of the hardness of the human heart. Thus, God allowed divorce but it was not His intention when He created marriage.

Though African-Americans have suffered under the misuse of the Bible, it is important to not blame the Bible, but the culprits of its misuse. Proper interpretation can explain parts of the Bible that appear to contradict God's character. Think about it this way, any misinterpretation of the Bible is a user error and not an error in the Bible itself.

REFLECTION QUESTIONS:

How has the Bible been used to marginalize and dehumanize African Americans?

___

___

___

Find one passage of Scripture that appears to promote sexism, classism, or racism. How can Dr. McCaulley's interpretive tool help you better understand that passage?

___

___

___

___

 WHAT DOES THIS MEAN FOR APOLOGETICS?

Now that we've affirmed the Bible's authority, how should that impact our reading of it? Here are a few practices to consider in our Bible interpretation.

---

26. Esau McCaulley, *Reading While Black: African American Biblical Interpretation As An Exercise in Hope* (Illinois: Intervarsity Press, 2020), 141.

Can We Trust the Bible? 25

1. **Recognize your humanity.**

   We are each shaped by our social and cultural context and this can impact our interpretation. However, this doesn't mean that reading Scripture will never lead you to any universal conclusions. For example, the idea that man is sinful and Jesus saves are universal truths. Who we are shapes how we approach the Bible, the concerns we take to the text, and inclines us to certain interpretations. It is our duty, as best we can, to acknowledge we never approach the text as black canvases. We must be aware of our cultural and biographical influences and work diligently to ensure they don't dominate our interpretation of the text.

2. **Recognize the Bible as a Story.**

   In college, I mostly attended topical Bible studies. While topical studies are insightful and can teach us much about the Bible, the Bible is a story composed of many themes and ideas that are best explained within the narrative. Think about a puzzle. It's nice to see portions of the puzzle, but we are more likely to misplace pieces if the puzzle is incomplete. The full picture is only realized when all the pieces are together. Looking at the full story of the Bible and understanding parts in light of the whole will keep us from misinterpreting passages in the Bible.

3. **Read the Bible in its Context.**

   The social/historical context of the Bible is important to interpretation. Whenever we see a news report on television, the reporter often takes us back to the scene of the event and provides important details. They do this to allow us to draw proper conclusions and fully understand what happened. When we read the Bible's story we need to act like news reporters searching for the social, cultural, and historical context so that we can understand the scene, draw the right conclusions, and give accurate explanations.

4. **Identify Prescriptive and Descriptive Texts.**

   The Bible is composed of *prescriptive* and *descriptive* texts. The prescriptive text refers to texts that prescribe a principle or command for humans to follow. For example, Micah 6:8 is a prescriptive text. Micah tells us that God requires us "to do justice, to love kindness, and to walk humbly with your God."

Descriptive texts describe historical events, contexts, and cultures. For example, 2 Samuel 13 describes the horrible rape of Tamar and 1 Samuel 17 explains how David defeats Goliath. They do not encourage rape or instruct us to kill a giant with a rock.

Determining if a text is descriptive versus prescriptive keeps us from misapplying passages and attempting to emulate everything we read.

5. **Interpret in Community.**

One of the errors of 21st century Christianity is interpreting Scripture in isolation. Communal interpretation includes having conversation partners with Christians throughout history, commentaries, theological resources and a loving local churches. Although God does illuminate the biblical text to individuals through His Holy Spirit, he has also given us the help of brothers and sisters to round out our interpretation and to protect us from unnecessary errors.

REFLECTION QUESTIONS:

Which of the practices above do you find most helpful?

_____
_____
_____

Are there any practices you would add?

_____
_____
_____
_____

CHAPTER THREE:
IS JESUS THE ONLY WAY?

Written By Yana Jenay Conner

Introduction

My friends jokingly call me a coffee house missionary. Just about every time I share a story about an opportunity I had to share the gospel or have a spiritual conversation, it begins with: "This one time when I was at a coffee shop..." I honestly don't know how this continues to happen, my introverted and shy self is usually uninterested in starting up a conversation with strangers. But, God always seems to have different plans.

One of these coffee shop encounters started by asking the lady close to me for the shop's internet password. She shared the password, but also went on to share her life story, including her struggles with same-sex attraction. After surrendering her life to the Lord, she stopped having relationships with women but struggled to recover from how she was treated by people in the church.

She energetically shared how Christ saved her from her sins, but as we continued, I noticed she started to make statements that sounded contradictory. For example, she said, "I believe all a person needs to do to get to heaven is be a good person."

I responded by asking, "If that's true, why do you need to be saved? Why did Christ die on a cross and pay the penalty for your sins if all you have to do to get to heaven is be a good person?"

She responded, "Well, this is the way for me. I believe there are

multiple ways to get to God."
I took a deep breath, said a quick prayer to settle my fear, and responded, "If God is a person with likes, dislikes, and a personality, then one person can't say 'He's this way,', and another says, 'No, he's this way,' and both be true. Would you agree?"

She tentatively nodded yes.

Continuing, I said, "Every religion has a different opinion on who God is and how to get to Him, but if God is a person with likes, dislikes, and a personality, like you and me, then someone is wrong. The only way to determine what is true is to go to the source. I believe that source is God's Word - the Bible."

To this, she responded, "Well, how do we know that the Bible is true? It was written so many years ago. God would have to come down and tell us that it's true for us to be able to trust it."

Before I could respond, she chuckled to herself and said, "Well, I guess He already did that, huh? Jesus, right?"

After joining her in laughter, our conversation gradually came to an end. I'd like to believe we both left the conversation more contemplative about what we believe and why we believe it. I left the conversation thinking about how the Bible shapes what I believe about salvation, sexuality, justice, and eternity.

Like my friend at the coffee shop, when we question Scripture's infallibility and trustworthiness, we create more questions than answers. For example, if we reject the Bible's profession that Christ is the only way and instead propose that a person simply has to be a good person to gain God's salvation, we leave a lot of questions on the table. Questions like:

1. Are there other paths to salvation?
2. How can we be sure these alternate paths will lead to Him?
3. What is "good" and when have we reached the level that will allow us to spend eternity with God?
4. How do we reconcile Jesus' claim, "I am the way, the truth, and the life. No one comes to the Father except through me (John 14:6)?" Is Jesus lying or leaving something out? If he's lying, is he still the perfect and spotless sacrifice for our sins?

Though questioning the infallibility of the Bible creates an intellectual conundrum, it's not the primary reason I propose we accept the Bible as infallible and trustworthy. As we learned in the last chapter, we can trust the Bible because "God came down" in the form of Christ and professed the Bible to be the truth about himself and his ways.

> "We can trust the Bible because 'God came down' in the form of Christ and professed the Bible to be the truth..."

This chapter will review the various ways people answer the question, "do all roads lead to heaven?" and provide an apologetic view that salvation is through Christ alone, based on His profession that He is the way, the truth, and the life (John 14: 3).

At the end of the lesson, you'll be able to answer the following questions:

1. What are the four different views on how a person can receive God's salvation and spend eternity with Him?

2. Which of these four views is biblical and why?

3. How does our belief in the Bible's infallibility and trustworthiness impact our formation of Christian doctrine?

4. What makes it difficult for people to accept exclusivity?

5. How does God's character help us navigate questions the Bible doesn't clearly answer?

Glossary (In Order of Appearance)

- **Universalism:** The belief that Christ's work on the cross was sufficient for the salvation of all humanity and that all are saved whether or not they confess Christ or any other religion.

- **Pluralism:** The belief that all religions teach the same thing, and therefore, any religion (or road) gives access to God and his salvation.

- **Inclusivism:** The belief that salvation comes through Christ, but it is possible for people to come to Christ outside of professing Jesus as Lord.

- **Exclusivism:** The belief that salvation comes through Christ alone and by faith in Jesus is the only way to God and his salvation.

A LOOK AT THE PAST

Throughout history, there have been four major views on how a person gains access to God and spends eternity with Him. The first is *universalism*, which believes that Christ's work on the cross was sufficient for the salvation of all of humanity and that everyone is saved whether or not they confess Christ or follow other faiths and religions. This conclusion is drawn from verses like John 3:16, which reads, "For God so loved the world that he gave his only son that whosoever believes in Him will not perish but have everlasting life." Though the latter part of this verse states that those who believe in Christ will not perish, universalists focus on the beginning of the verse. So, the universalists suggest that if Jesus died for the sins of the whole world, then all of humanity's sin debt is paid.

They believe it would be unjust for God to require Christ to die for the sins of all humanity but then only accept Christ's death for those who have faith in Him. In other words, belief is a requirement for salvation and would be a waste of the blood Christ shed. As a result, they conclude that no one needs a road to God because God has done all the work himself in Christ.

Faith is not required.

Pluralism, on the other hand, suggests that faith is needed for salvation, but that all religions teach the same thing. Therefore **any** religion or road will grant you access to God and his salvation.

A more nuanced application of pluralism is *inclusivism* which "insists that salvation is only through Jesus Christ or the church, but there may be people who are Christians without being consciously involved in Christianity."[27] When those who hold to this view read Jesus' statement that no one can come to the Father except through him and ask "what does it mean to come to Jesus?" and "does a person have to come to Jesus by professing faith in His name or can they come to him by embodying Christ's love ethic?" *Inclusivism* does not define any other way a person can come to faith and believes it is necessary to affirm the possibility that faith in Christ is shown by the many people

---

27. Millard Erickson, *Christian Theology*, ed. 3 (Grand Rapid, MI: Baker Academic) 2013, 814.

who embody Christ's love ethic, apart from faith in him.[28] One of the key text to support this argument is Matthew 7:18-23, which says,

> A good tree can't produce bad fruit; neither can a bad tree produce good fruit. Every tree that doesn't produce good fruits is cut down and thrown in the fire. So you'll recognize them by their fruit.

Based on this teaching, inclusivists argue that the ethics of one's life carries more weight than the profession of one's faith. Inclusivists believe that if a person embodies Christ's command to love their neighbor, it is possible for them to be a Christian without professing the name of Christ.

In stark contrast to the previous views, *exclusivism* affirms faith in Jesus as the **only** means for salvation and access to God (John 14: 6). Since the Jude 3 Project's belief is that exclusivism is the biblical position, we will discuss this in the next section.

REFLECTION QUESTIONS:

In your own words, summarize the four views of salvation presented in this section?

_____
_____
_____
_____

Which view is the most compelling to you and why?

_____
_____
_____
_____

---

28. See The Jude 3 Project, "Exclusivity vs. Inclusivity: Is Jesus the Only Way?," November 17, 2018, 51:10, https://youtu.be/2zswFQ0Vacw.

WHAT DOES THE BIBLE SAY

Although it would be enough, our acceptance of exclusivism is based on more than Jesus' profession that He is the only way to God. We also encounter themes in both the Old and New Testaments that point to a God who calls people to himself.

The Old Testament:

- God sets Noah apart and saves him from the damnation of the flood. (Genesis 6:9-8:22).
- God then calls Abram, aka Abraham, to leave his country and live in a foreign land where God promises to make Abram into a great nation that would be more numerous than the stars in the sky (Genesis 12:1-3,15:5).
- God uses his prophet, Moses, to deliver Abraham's descendants, Israel, from captivity in Egypt to be a nation unto himself (Exodus 1:1 -14:31).

In the New Testament, Jesus calls men and women to respond to his message through repentance and faith. Jesus' message was clear; He is the Messiah, the Son of God who had come to take away the sins of the world (Mark 2:17; Luke 5:31, 19:10). However, his salvific work on the cross was an invitation.
In Luke's gospel, Jesus likens the Kingdom of God to a banquet in which the master of the house invited his neighbors to join in on his feast (Luke 14:15-23). "Without exception," everyone who was invited came up with a reason for why they couldn't attend (Luke 14:18). In response, the master sent out a massive all-call to any and all who would come and share in his feast. Jesus concluded his parable, saying, "For I tell you, not one of those people who were invited will enjoy my banquet." In this parable, Jesus is communicating that his invitation into the Kingdom is for everyone, but only those who accept it will enter.

This parable, John 3:16, and many other Scriptures teach that only those who believe in Jesus will not perish. This debunks the universalist's view that salvation is given to everyone, regardless if they believe in Christ or not. Yes, Jesus died for the sins of the whole world and paid off the sin debt of every believer, but we only become a beneficiary of his work by receiving God's gracious gift through faith.

To emphasize that salvation is exclusively for those who receive Christ's invitation and not universal, Christ collectively refers to those who put their faith in him as the Church. As we noted earlier, the Bible was originally written in Hebrew, Aramaic, and Greek. The Greek term *ekklesia* translates to church which means "called out ones."[29] With the use of this term, Jesus acknowledges that there will be some who receive his invitation and some will not. There will be some that are called out because of their faith and others that are not because of their disbelief.

Additionally, in Ephesians 2, Paul describes salvation as a gift received by faith, not works. He writes, "For you are saved by grace through faith, and this is not from yourselves; it is God's gift--not from works, so that no one can boast" (Ephesians 2:8-9). The profession of the totality of Scripture is that salvation is by grace through faith, not works—not being a good person.

REFLECTION QUESTIONS:

Why is it important to understand what the Bible teaches about eternity?

What other passages of Scriptures communicate that salvation is by grace through faith?

---

29. As defined by the Strong Concordance, *ekklsía*, is from a compound of ek and a derivative of *kale* which means to call out of. However, the popular meeting, especially a religious congregation, is assembly or church.

WHAT MAKES EXCLUSIVISM DIFFICULT TO ACCEPT?

There are at least three common reasons people tend to reject exclusivism:

1. The Term "Exclusivity". Let's be honest, the term exclusivity is not endearing. It sounds cliquish and elitist. It seems like Christians are bouncers standing outside of the church deciding who can and cannot come in. However, this is not the case. God decides who can enter into his Kingdom. It's his kingdom! Though people may perceive exclusivists to be prideful, the opposite is true. We are inclusive in that we share the gospel with any and all who will receive Christ's invitation of salvation, and we are humble in acknowledging that we don't make the rules. We are mere ambassadors of Christ's message of salvation (2 Corinthians 5:20-21). We are like the servants who go out to the highways and byways, looking for those who will come and share in the master's feast (Luke 14:23).

2. The Reality of Hell and Character of God. Hell and the character of God, are closely related theological concepts. Many struggle to reconcile the idea of a loving God casting humans into hell whether they are "good" or "bad" people by our definition. Though I wholeheartedly understand their struggles and have wrestled with them as well, the Bible offers the following to help shape the way we engage with this issue:

- **This is Our Father's World:** We are not the first to wrestle with these questions. In the book of Romans, Paul writes to Christians with similar concerns who believed God to be unjust in saving some and not all. In response to questioning God's goodness, Paul writes, "But who are you, a mere [hu]man, to talk back to God? Will what is formed say to the one who formed it, 'Why did you make me like this? Or has the potter no right over the clay, to make from the same lump one piece of pottery of honor and another for dishonor (Romans 9:20-21)?'" In essence, Paul is saying, "Since God is the Creator of all things, He can do whatever He desires to do. He is Lord. Who are we to question his ways?"

This is a difficult reality to come to grips with, but this is our Father's world and He rules over it as He chooses. His ways are not our ways and His thoughts are not like ours (Isaiah 55:8-9). However, we can trust that his thoughts and his ways are always good and formed out of his love for us.

- **God's Love is Holy and Just:** God is the definition of love, and his love is both holy and just. In love, He punishes sin. To not punish sin would make him unjust. However, it's important to remember that in his love He has made a way for all to respond to him by sending Christ into the world to die for our sins. All who believe in Him can experience his salvation.

> "Because God is holy, His definition of good is often different than ours."

- **Our Definition of Good is Different Than God's**: Because God is holy, His definition of good is different from ours. Paul states that every human being on the planet falls short of his definition of good (Romans 3:23). Even our best works are tainted and appear before him as filthy rags, which means though our works may be good, they aren't good enough to make us right with God (Isaiah 64:6). Only Jesus can do that (Romans 3:21-26).

REFLECTION QUESTION:
Besides the reasons stated in this section, what are other reasons exclusivism may be difficult to accept? How would you respond to these objections from the Bible?

_____
_____
_____
_____

WHAT DOES THIS MEAN FOR APOLOGETICS?

Like everything we've discussed in this book so far, our goal is to equip you to have meaningful, God-honoring conversations with others for the sake of the gospel. Our purpose is not to help you build an arsenal of information so you can cleverly "win" a debate. A "win" is not looking smart or poking holes in someone else's view, leaving them looking stupid or confused. A win is gaining a brother or sister in Christ. A win is being able to provide a defense for Jesus' truth claim that He is the way, the truth, and the life. Therefore, keep the following in mind when conversing with others about salvation and eternity:

- **Fall in Love with the Gospel.** Let your love for the gospel that has saved you fuel your desire to defend it from error.

- **Trust the Spirit.** In Acts 1:8, Jesus tells his disciples that they will receive empowerment from the Spirit to be his witnesses in all the earth. Though apologetics can appear to be a discipline focused solely on mental effort, it is ultimately the work of the Spirit. Our arguments don't save people, the Spirit does. Therefore pray often for the Spirit's empowerment.

- **Be Okay With Unanswered Questions**. One of the critiques of the exclusivist view is that it doesn't account for people who have not heard the gospel. How can God hold them accountable for what they don't know? Honestly, this question has kept me up some nights. However, because the Bible doesn't offer a clear answer to this question, we can only "rock with" what we know and believe to be the best of our God. What we know is that salvation is by grace through faith and that our God is loving, holy, wise, and good. Therefore, we can trust that He has done what is loving, holy, wise, and good by making the road to salvation through Christ.

REFLECTION QUESTIONS:

What questions does this chapter prompt you to ask?

_____
_____
_____
_____

Where can you find the answers to your questions in God's Word?

_____
_____
_____
_____

On a personal level, what questions go unanswered that lead you to trust in the character of God?

_____
_____
_____
_____

CHAPTER FOUR:
WHAT IS SIN?

Written By Yana Jenay Conner

Introduction

Shortly after God uttered the words "it is very good" over his creation, his goodness was called into question. The serpent planted into Eve's mind the idea that the One who had given her everything was actually keeping something good from her.

The truth is, God *was* keeping something from Eve. But it wasn't something good—it was the knowledge of evil. While Adam and Eve had an all-access pass to the tree of life, God commanded them to abstain from eating from the tree of the knowledge of good and evil. They intimately knew what was good through God and his creation, but God never wanted them to encounter evil.

But tempted by the devil, Eve looked at the fruit hanging from the tree of knowledge of good and evil and decided that it was "*good* for food and delightful to look at" and "desirable for obtaining wisdom" (Genesis 3:6). Eve approached the forbidden tree, raised her arm to grab hold of its ripest offering, put the fruit to her mouth, and ate. Then she shared it with her husband, Adam.

> **"That one act of disobedience plunged the world into sin and misery."**
>
> **Charles Octavious Boothe,**
> *Plain Theology for Plain People*

And just like that, sin entered the world, and everything that was once declared good began to unravel. Adam and Eve hid from God. God confronted Adam. Adam blamed Eve. God confronted Eve. Eve blamed creation. In an instant, God's relationship with humanity and humanity's relationship with itself and creation became tainted and broken by *sin*. As theologian Charles Octavius Boothe puts it, "That one act of disobedience plunged the world into sin and misery."[30]

Every day we experience this sin and misery. We experience it in our bodies, hearts, minds, relationships, and communities. Sin, as many theologians have explained, is pervasive, meaning there is not one aspect of life that sin has not touched.[31]

In this chapter, we are going to discuss two views on the source of sin, compare each view to what the Bible teaches about sin, and consider why our understanding of sin matters as we seek to be faithful apologists.

---

30. Boothe, Charles Octavius, Plain Theology for Plain People (Bellingham, WA: Lexham Press, 2007), 29.
31. Fields, Bruce L., *Introducing Black Theology: Three Crucial Questions for the Evangelical Church* (Grand Rapids, MI: Baker Academic, 2001.

At the end of the lesson, you'll be able to answer the following questions:

1. What are the two views concerning the source of sin?

2. What is individual sin?

3. What is systemic sin?

4. Does the Bible teach that sin is individual, systemic, or both?

5. How are individual sin and systemic sin different from one another?

6. How do individual sin and systemic sin work together?

7. How does one's view of sin impact their understanding of the Church's role in the **world**?

Glossary (In Order of Appearance

- **Sin:** Disobedience to God's commands. However, this disobedience is likely rooted in some kind of idolatry.

- **Systematic Theology:** A topical approach to understanding the core doctrines of the Bible (i.e. God, creation, salvation, sin, etc.).

- **Evangelicalism:** "A movement of gospel centrality, focused on the primacy of Scripture and justification by faith that emerged from the reformation."

- **Individualism:** A worldview in which the individual and individuality are the most valued entities of the society.

- **Individual Racism:** Racism that is the "result of individuals choosing to act in a racist manner."

- **Systemic Racism:** Racism perpetuated by society even if individuals in society do not intend to be racist.

 ## A LOOK AT THE PAST

There are various questions surrounding the doctrine of sin, such as its nature, results, and magnitude. In this lesson, we are going to discuss two views concerning sin's source. In essence, we are asking the question: Where does sin reside?

In his *systematic theology* textbook, *Christian Theology*, Dr. Millard J. Erickson explains that some believe sin to be individualistic, meaning sin solely or primarily resides in and springs from the person. He writes, "In the traditional understanding, sin is often seen as a matter of the individual's broken relationship with God; thus sin is basically unbelief, rebellion or somthing of that type."[32] To put it another way, the individualistic view reads the Genesis 3 account and primarily considers how sin impacted a person's relationship with God, not their relationship with others and creation. In addition to this explanation of the traditional views of sin, Erickson adds, "individual sin has often been the major object of attention for evangelical Christians" in which "sin and salvation are considered matters pertaining strictly to individual human beings."[33]

This view of sin is a direct result of *evangelicalism* being born and raised in a Western society that is built on *individualism*. In *Misreading Scripture with Western Eyes,* E. Randolph Richards and Brandon J. O'Brien provide insight into the mind of Western society's individualism, writing,

> Western societies are, by and large, individualistic societies. The most important entity in an individualistic culture is the individual person. The person's identity comes by distinguishing herself from the people around her. She is encouraged to avoid peer pressure and be an independent thinker. She will make her decisions regardless of what others think; she may defy her parents with her choice of a college major, career, or spouse. The highest goal and virtue in this sort of culture is being true to oneself. The supreme value is the sovereignty of the individual.[34]

It is this individualistic perspective that not only impacts one's view of sin but also informs one's emphasis on personal salvation. When an evangelical encounters the brokenness of the world, they conclude that the solution is primarily "saving souls." The logic is that as you save souls, the brokenness in the world will fade away.

Another outcome of individualism's impact on views of sin is relativistic constructions of sin, in which people define sin for themselves apart from biblical or authoritative teachings. This merger of individualism and relativism has led many to redefine what constitutes as sin in relation to sexuality, justice, and a

---
32. Erickson, Millard J., *Christian Theology,* ed. 3 (Grand Rapids, MI: Baker Academic, 2013), 539.
33. Ibid., 585.
34. Richards, E. Randolph and O'Brien, Brandon J., *Misreading Scripture with Western Eyes: Removing Cultural Blinders to Better Understand the Bible* (Downers Grove, IL: InterVarsity Press, 2012, 96.

host of other lifestyle choices. At this present moment, our culture seems to primarily understand sin as a grievance against neighbor, not God. This outlook can be summed up in statements such as, "As long as I'm not hurting anybody" or "love is love, not sin." However, this definition of sin is an overemphasis on the second greatest commandment to love thy neighbor with little to no regard for the first commandment's call to love the Lord with all one's heart, soul, mind, and strength (Matthew 22:36-40).

In contrast to the individualistic view of sin is the systemic view, which was popularized by James Cone, J. Deotis Roberts, and other proponents of Black theology. Summarizing Black theology and its definition of systemic sin, Dr. Bruce Fields writes,

> Black theology as a movement reminds the church of the pervasiveness of sin in systems, structures, and sociopolitical institutions. *Systematic sin* should be thought of as the bentness of the human nature manifested in the perpetuation of injustice to, and the dehumanization of, select groups in socio-cultural constructs."[35]

In short, Black theology concludes that sin resides not only in humans but also in the systems and structures humans create. The concept of systematic sin assumes that broken people produce broken structures. The same is true in regards to racism in which racist people create racist structures. Therefore, racism is both *individual and systemic*. If this is true, then not only do racist people need salvation and redemption, but the structures they create need salvation and redemption as well. With this in mind, they conclude that "saving souls" is not enough, and the Church needs to prioritize making disciples *and* doing justice. Both are critical.

Though Black theology acknowledges the reality of sin existing in both the individual and the structures they have a tendency to overemphasize the reality of systematic sin to ensure its implications don't get lost. However, as we will see in the next section, the Bible presents evidence for both views and calls Christians to pursue the redemption of individuals and systems equally.

---

35. Fields, 67-68.

💭 REFLECTION QUESTIONS:

Do you tend to think of sin as primarily individual or systemic? What do you think influences your views?

_____

_____

_____

How would you respond to someone who says, "As long as I'm not hurting anybody, there isn't anything sinful about what I'm doing?"

_____

_____

_____

_____

WHAT DOES THE BIBLE SAY?

It's not really too much of a stretch for people to believe that sin is individual. We sin every day. For example, in the garden, it was *Eve* who determined in *her* heart that the fruit of the tree of the knowledge of good and evil was "good" for food and wisdom, and then "took some of its fruit and ate it." And it was *Adam* who then followed suit.

From Genesis onward, men and women rejected God's definition of what is good and determined what was "good" for themselves. Cain, Abram, Sarah, Joseph's brothers, Pharaoh, Moses, King Saul, King David, and all the kings and generations that followed did something of the sort.

And today when someone commits a crime, *they*, not the systems and structures around them, are imprisoned. Even if the systems and structures played a significant role in the individual's decisions, people, not systems, are held accountable and bear the consequences.

Therefore, the question before us is: Does the Bible provide any evidence for systematic sin?

In Romans 12:1-2, Paul compels his brothers and sisters in Christ to present their lives as a living sacrifice. He even tells them how to do it, writing, "Do not conform to the pattern of this world but be transformed by the renewing of your mind" (Romans 12:2, NIV). With these words, Paul is suggesting that there is a "pattern of the world" that stands in opposition to God's "good, pleasing and perfect will."

Paul speaks similarly of the systemic presence of sin in the world in his letter to the church at Ephesus and Colossae. To the church at Ephesus, he writes about how they used to live "according to the ways of the world," but now, because of their new position in Christ, they have been liberated from this way of life and empowered to live in a new way (Ephesians 2:1-7). To Colossae, Paul warns them against being taken captive by "philosophy and empty deceit based on human tradition, based on the elements of the world, rather than Christ" (Colossians 2:8). Paul adds to this warning that Jesus came not only to cancel our individual sin debts but also to disarm the spiritual rulers and authorities that lurk in the systems and patterns of the world (Colossians 2:14).

On the surface, these systems present themselves in the lack of equal pay based on ethnicity and gender, mass incarceration of black men in comparison to their white counterparts, redlining, and gentrification that continue to push those below the poverty line out of their homes, slavery, and it's relentless twin, racism. However, as stated in Field's definition, systemic sin is "the bentness of human nature manifested in the perpetuation of injustice to, and the dehumanization of, select groups in socio-cultural constructs." If this is true, what is the bentness of human nature that creates unjust systems of these kinds? Erickson defines this bentness as idolatry. He writes, "Idolatry in any form…is the essence of sin." I wholeheartedly agree with his conclusion and would add that this idolatry is an idolatry of the self.

For example, as my good friend Josh Reed helped me understand, we see self-preservation at the root of so many instances of sin in the Bible. Consider Abram before he was father Abraham. On two occasions he lied about his relationship with his wife, Sarai, to preserve his life. Sarai was a stone-cold Jewish fox and he knew men would be after her so when they entered a new city, he would tell everyone she was his sister. He was sure he would be killed if he said he was her husband. What a guy!

If we look closer, we realize that there are some systemically sinful realities that influenced Abram's individual sin. One being, his culture's value of men over women which convinced Abram his well-being was more important than Sarai's. The other, the pattern of women being treated as commodities instead of human beings which fueled Abram's fear that any man more powerful than him could just take his wife if he wanted her. Here, Abram's individual desire to preserve his well-being partners with the systemic realities of his day, leading him to sin.

Then there is Pharaoh who, after noticing the Israelites were beginning to outnumber the Egyptians, sought to enslave them to preserve his power and the superiority of his people (Exodus 1:8-14). His bentness led to 400 years of dehumanization and enslavement of an entire people group. Sound familiar? 400 years of slavery? The dehumanization and enslavement of an entire people group? Could it be that self-preservation is what fuels slavery and causes so many to hold racist ideals of white supremacy? Could it also be self-preservation that causes a number of evangelicals, particularly white ones, to emphasize individual racism over systemic racism? Because they know acknowledging systemic racism would require them to do something about it, and relinquish some of the privileges they would prefer to preserve.

As we will see in the next section, it's this kind of unholy self-preservation, along with a host of others, that have caused so many to struggle with Christians and reject Christianity.

REFLECTION QUESTIONS:

What are other examples of individual and systemic sin in Scripture?

_____

_____

_____

_____

How do you see self-preservation playing out in the heart of individuals and systems in our society?

_____

_____

_____

_____

HOW HAS THIS DOCTRINE BEEN MISUSED?

Both evangelicals and Black theologians would agree to some extent that sin is both individual and systemic. However, evangelicals tend to view sin as primarily individual while Black theologians can overemphasize the reality of systematic sin. This imbalance has created more of an ethical debate than a theological one as each group defines the role of the Church in the world in fulfilling the Great Commission.

Evangelicals tend to conclude the primary role of Christians and the Church is to convert sinners. Their view of salvation and the gospel is centered around the transformation of the individual. As Erickson explains, because evangelicals believe "the unit of morality is the individual person," their goal is the "regeneration" of individuals.[36] They believe that as people are regenerated, systems will be regenerated as well.

However, proponents of Black theology believe the systemic issues plaguing the world require a more dynamic evangelism strategy that includes turning over systems of injustice. They would conclude we need not only regeneration but also reform.

---

36. Erickson, 597.

> "The Spirit of the Lord is on me, because he has anoited me to preach the good news to the poor, he has sent me to proclaim release to the captives and recovery of sight to the blind, to set free the oppressed, to proclaim the year of the Lord's favor."
>
> **Jesus,** Luke 4:18-19

Yes, we need to go, therefore, but we also need to teach people how to obey Christ's commands, which include love for your neighbor, doing justice, and loving mercy (Micah 6:8; Matthew 22:39). This, too, is the Church's responsibility. Especially since Jesus has made it clear that when he comes back the question will not be how many souls we fed, but how many mouths we fed, how many bodies we clothed, and how many prisoners we visited (Matthew 25:31-46).

For onlookers, watching the church battle about whether we need to "just preach the gospel" or "preach a just gospel" has left a bitter taste in their mouths. They don't understand why such a divide exists. Additionally, evangelicals (specifically white evangelicals) de-emphasis on sociocultural and political issues has created a barrier to many's acceptance of Christ. They have painted a picture of a Jesus who is more concerned with them living right than being whole. However, this stands in contrast to the picture of Jesus painted in the Scriptures. In his inaugural address, Jesus proclaimed, "The Spirit of the Lord is on me, because he has anointed me to preach the good news to the poor, he has sent me to proclaim release to the captives and recovery of sight to the blind, to set free the oppressed, to proclaim the year of the Lord's favor (Luke 4:18-19)." Jesus' mission was to preach the gospel and set people free from sinful and oppressive systems. To follow him is to do the same. It is so essential for the Church to recapture and embody Christ's mission.

WHAT DOES THIS MEAN FOR APOLOGETICS?

Divisiveness is unfortunate. Especially when there is no need for it to exist. And since the Bible teaches the existence of both individual and systemic sin, there is no need for the dichotomy or division. Therefore, as apologists, our objectives are two-fold:

1. **Be Balanced in Our Presentation of the Gospel:** We need to preach a gospel that brings attention to the individual and systemic realities of sin and to Jesus Christ, who has come to redeem and renew both. When we preach a gospel devoid of the realities of systemic sin, we promote an individualistic view of Christianity that ignores God's command for us to love our neighbor as ourselves and to do justice in the world. When we share the gospel we want people to know that they have not only been saved from something but that they have also been saved *to* something. Saved from sin and saved to usher in God's just and equitable kingdom.

2. **Follow Christ in Word and Deed:** Let your life, not only your words, be an apologetic for the gospel. We testify to the character of God when we embody his just and compassionate character in the world. As you preach and defend the gospel, also be a faithful servant that uses your time and talent in your community for the benefit of others.

REFLECTION QUESTIONS:

What is your biggest takeaway from this lesson?

_____
_____
_____

How can you follow Christ in both word and deed in your community? What talents has God given you for the benefit of others?

_____
_____
_____
_____

CHAPTER FIVE:
WHAT IS JUSTICE?

Written By Sherelle Ducksworth

Introduction

I still remember the first time I experienced unfair treatment. I was in kindergarten, and a classmate accused me of cheating in a Sesame Street card game. The teacher quickly sided with my accuser and punished me without giving me an opportunity to share my side of the story. This wasn't the last time I experienced unfair treatment. As a matter of fact, I later learned about injustices much more serious than my Sesame Street debacle. Between growing up in the Mississippi Delta and attending an HBCU, I have spent most of my life learning about the injustices black people have experienced and the legacy of activism and protest we have built by demanding justice and demonstrating what justice looks like.

In secular spaces, conclusions on what justice looks like often takes the form of *utilitarianism* or *social justice*. Utilitarianism aims to implement actions that bring the most happiness, usefulness, and benefits for the greatest number of people in a society. For example, eminent domain is arguably a form of utilitarianism. Eminent domain is when the government confiscates private property in order to produce something for society as a whole. In short, it seeks to do what is best for a large group of people as opposed to one individual.

Social justice is a broad concept with a number of definitions that encourage equality, fairness, and equity in society. Social justice relies on secular theories and philosophies about what is right, fair, and equitable in society. However, it is important to note that for some, social justice literally means justice in society. This is something the Bible speaks passionately about and is therefore not immediately contradictory to the Bible.

To many Christians, justice originates from God and the Bible is the primary source for understanding justice. The Bible has three words for justice: *tsedeq, mishpat,* and *dikaios.* These words refer to justice both as a verb meaning to do what is right, fair, and equitable, and as an adjective referring to being righteous, fair, or just. Unlike utilitarianism and secular social justice, biblical justice is rooted in the character of God and his Word, not secular theories, philosophies, or societal utility. This distinction, however, does not mean that secular understandings of justice offer no benefit to the way Christians think about justice. They do. It just means the Bible is the ultimate authority over our conclusions about justice.

At the end of the lesson, you'll be able to answer the following questions:

1. How does the Bible define justice?

2. What are two secular ways of identifying what is just?

3. What is God's providence and sovereignty?

4. How have African American Christians understood justice?

Glossary (In Order of Appearance

- **Utilitarianism–**The idea that actions are just and ethical when they produce happiness or benefits for the greatest number of people.

- **Social Justice–**On a basic level, social justice is the pursuit of equity and fairness in society. Social justice is a broad concept that means different things to different people and should be clearly defined before being used by Christians.

- **Biblical Justice–**Justice rooted in the character of God that encourages humans' relationships with God and one another to be right, fair, and equitable. Justice is both a verb and an adjective and functions both individually and institutionally.

- **Divine Sovereignty–**God is the supreme authority and Lord over all things, which means that nothing happens unless God causes it or allows it.

- **Providence–**God cares for, preserves, and governs creation to ensure the execution of his divine will.

- **Vice-regents–**a person who serves as a ruler or lord over something on behalf of another.

- **Theocracy–**an earthly government ruled by a king or priest appointed by God.

👀 A LOOK AT THE PAST

Historically for African American Christians, justice has had spiritual and earthly relevance. "Spiritual" refers to their righteous standing before God given through salvation, and "earthly" refers to the command to live righteously on the earth. Their commitment to display righteousness in society was never detached from their spiritual need for righteousness. Many saw their pursuit of earthly justice as a result of their salvation. Justice concerned both personal liberation from sin and the command that Christians *do* justice in the world.

However, the Black experience in America required a louder public proclamation of earthly liberation. Therefore, African Americans prioritized earthly justice in their public theology. In other words, while black people affirmed and preached about the need for spiritual liberation, the public outcry was overwhelmingly about physical liberation. This emphasis on physical liberation can be seen across four historical eras including, slavery, Jim Crow, Civil Rights, and post-Civil Rights. In this chapter, we will briefly explore how Christian theologians and activists understood justice to have social implications.

From the 1600's through the late 1800's, black abolitionists and preachers proclaimed messages of freedom and liberation from chattel slavery. Though some Christians rejected the abuses of slavery, pro-slavery Christians believed slavery was supported by the Bible. For example, Baptist preacher Richard Fuller rooted his sanctioned pro-slavery defense in the Scriptures and rejected claims that holding black people as slaves was a sin.[37]

On the contrary, African American Christian abolitionists and preachers took the Exodus liberation narrative in the Bible as affirmation that God's will included both spiritual and physical freedom and liberation. They advocated for the abolishment of slavery with a biblical conviction in slavery's unrighteousness and God's liberating power. For example, Henry Highland Garnet preached a gospel message that included physical freedom and liberation and worked adamantly for the abolishment of

---

37. Richard Fuller, *Domestic Slavery Considered as a Scriptural Institution*, eds. Nathan A. Finn and Keith Harper (Georgia: Mercer University Press, 2008), 7.

slavery.[38] Methodist pastor Daniel Payne preached for the abolition of slavery and argued that it was against the will of God.[39] Others such as James Pennington, Sojourner Truth, and Frederick Douglas also devoted themselves to speaking and preaching about the necessity of physical liberation in response to God's Word and God's moral law.

By the end of slavery, African Americans faced a new oppressive social system called Jim Crow, which separated black people from white people and produced social inequality, racism, and discrimination. Subsequently, justice conversations among African American Christians centered on the social, political, and economic disenfranchisement of black people. Similar to their predecessors, they made a connection between their fight and faith. They believed the gospel was inclusive of both physical and social liberation. For example, Fannie Lou Hamer saw a clear connection between Christianity and her fight for liberation. She frequently used the New Testament and the Exodus theme of liberation to support her fight for justice.[40] Martin Luther King Jr. preached a gospel inclusive of physical liberation.[41] He rooted his fight against *de facto* and *de jure* segregation in the transformative social ethic that the law of God and the life of Christ demonstrated.[42]

After the Civil Rights movement, black men and women began to reimagine the black agenda for justice in order to maintain a prophetic voice against the social ills that remained after the Civil Rights era. Today, in the midst of injustices such as police brutality and disparities in health care and education, pastors are casting a vision for justice that identifies justice as a combination of right belief and right action. Dr. Charlie Dates, pastor of Progressive Baptist Church, captured this 21st century vision

---

38. David Swift, *Black Prophets of Justice: Activist Clergy Before the Civil War* (Louisiana: Louisiana State University Press, 1989), 119-121.
39 Wayne E. Croft Sr., *The Motif of Hope in African American Preaching During Slavery and the Post-Civil War Era* (New York: Lexington Books, 2017), 77.
40. Rosetta E. Ross, *Witnessing & Testifying: Black Women, Religion, and Civil Rights* (Minneapolis: Fortress Press, 2003), 110-113
41. James H. Harris, *Preaching Liberation* (Minneapolis: Fortress Press, 1995), 54.
42. Kenyatta R. Gilbert, *A Pursued Justice: Black Preaching from the Great Migration to Civil Rights* (Texas: Baylor University Press, 2016), 107-109.

of justice in a sermon delivered at the 2018 MLK50 conference. Dates spoke of the relationship between justice and the gospel declaring, "to get the gospel right is to somehow move beyond the preservation of right doctrine to the place where we apply that right doctrine through the church's influence to the world around her to somehow make public the profession of her faith."[43][7]

Since the 1600's, African Americans have understood justice as an outcome of their Christian conversion and maintained the connection between the gospel and physical liberation. Though social ills differ across history and the strategies for attaining justice might differ among black people, African American Christians have maintained the significance of a connection between spiritual and physical liberation. Many continue to insist that the Christian faith is both word and deed.

REFLECTION QUESTIONS:

What are the possible consequences of using utilitarianism or secular social justice as primary sources for understanding justice?

_____

_____

_____

_____

What do the biblical words for justice, *tsedeq, mishpat,* and *dikaios*, reveal about biblical justice?

_____

_____

_____

_____

---

43. Dr. Charlie Dates, *"The Most Segregated Hour in America"*. MLK 50 Conference.

WHAT DOES THE BIBLE SAY?

As mentioned in the introduction, justice is both a verb and an adjective. Here is a summary of what the Old Testament teaches about *being just* and *doing justice*.

- In Genesis, God created a righteous world with righteous humans who were commanded to develop a righteous society. The fact that God called creation "good" lets us know that the world began as a just place (Genesis 1:31). God created humans as his image bearing *vice-regents* (Genesis 1:26, 28 and 2:15) and commissioned them to reflect his justice in their being, in relation to others, and in society.

- However, Adam's fall brought corruption which changed humanity from righteous to unrighteous. Unfortunately, Adam's fall corrupted the earthly kingdom of righteousness on earth. Consequently, humans became separated from God, sinful, and doers of unrighteousness (Genesis 4 and 6).

- Existing now without the ability to live justly on their own, God enabled the Israelites to *be just*, *do justice,* and to live in a just society by creating a *theocracy* for Israel. The Israelites received God's righteous standards that would allow them to live in relationship with God (Exodus 20:1-11; 23; 24; 25; Leviticus 4; 59; 26), with others (Exodus 20:12-17), and to maintain a just society (Exodus 20:12-17; 21; 22; Leviticus 25:23-55).

- However, Israel failed to live justly and evoked God's anger, judgment, and mercy. A number of prophets proclaimed God's judgment, anger, and command to do justice, some in direct reference to the oppressed, poor, widowed, and stranger (Isaiah 1:21-23; Jeremiah 22:3; Ezekiel 18, 22:1-7; Amos 5; Micah 6:7; Zechariah 7:9). The Old Testament ends with a promise of the coming Righteous One.

The New Testament continues the themes of *being just* and *doing justice* often using the words *righteous and justice* interchangeably. Beginning with the life of Jesus, the New Testament reveals:

- Jesus as the Righteous One (Acts 22:14) demonstrated how to *be just, do justice, and live justly* in His righteous relationship with God the Father (Matthew 4:17), humanity, and creation.
- Jesus *doing justice* in his care for the marginalized and condemning the exploitation of the vulnerable, poor, and widowed (Luke 11:37-54).
- Jesus fulfilled God's righteous standard for humanity, dying an atoning death, and providing humans with the ability to *be just* before God.

Jesus leaves his followers with three new ideas about righteousness:

- First, the *theocracy* is not an earthly reality. Instead, the kingdom of righteousness is an eternal reality imitated on earth through the Church (2 Peter 3:13). We see this in Paul's appeal for justice in Acts 22. After Paul was seized and beaten for his teaching in Jerusalem, he appealed to the stipulations of his Roman citizenship in accordance with their law and demanded he is treated justly. This is a clear example of a follower of Christ imitating the kingdom of righteousness by fighting for justice on earth.
- Secondly, individuals *become just* by their faith in Jesus' death on the cross (Galatians 3:8-13; Philippians 3:9; Titus 3:5; 1 Peter 2:23-24).
- Lastly, Christians are empowered by the Spirit of God to *do justice* in the world (Galatians 5:18; 6:8-10). The Church is meant to serve as a model of loving justice in the world. Paul emphasized the importance of love in giving to the poor in 1 Corinthians 13:3. He later commended the church at Macedonia for giving out of love and made a connection between giving to the needy and their righteousness (2 Corinthians 9:7-11). John identified righteousness as an outcome of love, those who practice righteousness as children of the Righteous One, and the organic nature of love as one that translates through actions (1 John 3:7, 11-

12, 18; 4:7). Thus, the Church is motivated by their love for God and others to *do justice.*

In light of the teachings in the New Testament, believers are *declared just* and admonished to actively *do justice* as they await their new residence in the eternal kingdom of righteousness.

> **REFLECTION QUESTIONS:**
>
> What stereotypes of the oppressed, foreigners, orphans, marginalized, and widows can hinder our ability to pursue justice for them?
>
> _____
> _____
> _____
> _____
>
> Why should Christian love be the foundation of *doing justice*?
>
> _____
> _____
> _____
> _____

 HOW HAS THIS DOCTRINE BEEN MISUSED?

Some African Americans struggle to see God as just because of our history of injustice. I have had black students ask me, "Why would I believe in a God that allowed American slavery?" Over the years, I have heard people try to answer this question three ways: First, some believe that societal injustice is not a gospel issue. Secondly, some deny that biblical justice is concerned with societal structures. And lastly, some highlight God's *providence* to explain injustice. How should we respond to these propositions?

Does justice relate to society?

As we observed in the previous section, biblical justice can be applied to the public sphere. This truth was demonstrated through the Old Testament *theocracy*, the Church's obligation to *do justice*, and Paul's appeal to justice in Acts 22. Though Christians await a coming kingdom of righteousness, the epistles consistently teach Christians to *do justly* now.

Does God cause injustice?

We want to be careful when we talk about God's providence in conversations about injustice. The truth is, injustice and God's providence exist in a tension we cannot fully explain. However, we do know that the evil in the world comes from the actions of humans and Satan, not God (James 1:13-15). Thus, we can conclude that God does not cause injustice or delight in injustice.

As children of God who live in the midst of injustice, we must remember that injustice is not a reflection of God, but a reflection of the total depravity of humanity. Additionally, we are called to not only be righteous in our individual lives but to seek to *do justice* in the public sphere. This is the fruit of our salvation.

 WHAT DOES THIS MEAN FOR APOLOGETICS?

Practically, what does this chapter encourage us to do? There are at least five ways Christians can respond:

1. **Emphasize the coming kingdom of righteousness**
   The overall story of the Bible is that a just God took on human flesh, becoming Jesus of Nazareth and dying on the cross on our behalf. He did this to enable us to be declared just before God. This eternal hope does not eradicate the earthly need for justice. Instead, it gives us hope to endure and work towards bringing about righteousness in a fallen world. This hope is what enabled our ancestors to continue their pursuit of justice in the midst of slavery and Jim Crow. When sharing the gospel, we recall the justice that is available to the world. Jesus pointed the poor, sick, oppressed, and marginalized to a greater kingdom where true righteousness reigns—especially in the midst of injustice. Tell the story of justice to those who suffer injustices, so that they might be convinced of the work of the Righteous One and join the family of God.

2. **Do justice and be just individually**

   In light of the life and ministry of the prophets, Jesus, and the apostles, it is clear that we are to *do justice* every day. As followers of Christ, we must bear the fruit of righteousness personally. We should be righteous persons who are self-controlled, kind, peaceful, hospitable, loving, patient, caring, slow to anger, humble, meek, and faithful. In our relationships, we are to be motivated by love to do what is right, fair, and equitable. We do not wait on systems, policies, or ministry functions to do what is right. Instead, in our individual lives as teachers, administrators, lawyers, cashiers, law enforcement, cafeteria workers, politicians, preachers, husbands, singles, grandparents, aunts, neighbors, and friends, we are to do what is right in our individual interactions with others.

   > "Our righteousness must be put into practice in the public space."

3. **Do justice in the public space**

   Our righteousness must be put into practice in the public space. God created humans to exist together in society with moral relationships filled with justice. One element of society is the social institutions intended to meet the basic needs of citizens. These institutions are created and operated by fallen persons, so it is inevitable that they include policies and systems that are not always right, fair, and equitable. Thus, individuals must call out injustices in society and work to reform those injustices and do what is right. Again, this is what Paul does in Acts 22 when he appeals to the Roman law for his personal justice. To be a follower of Yahweh is to be an advocate for justice. Become a participant in town hall meetings, run for office, serve on city boards, serve on committees in your job and at your child's school, and get involved in your community!

4. Disciple others to take up the mantle of justice

Justice is not merely something taken up by those with a special calling in law or politics. Instead, doing justice is a vital part of what it means to be a follower of Christ. In the Gospels, we observe Jesus being justice and renewal to the marginalized, establishing His kingdom of righteousness. If we are to imitate Jesus, and Jesus lived a life of *justice,* His followers are to *do justice* as well. A part of the Great Commission in Matthew 28:16-20 is to *teach them to observe all that I commanded you.* Thus, if Jesus commanded the disciples to help the vulnerable (Matthew 25:35-46; 26:11), then we are compelled to make disciples who actively follow in His footsteps and do what is right, just, and fair and plead with others to do the same.

REFLECTION QUESTIONS:

What are practical ways that you can act justly in your home and with your friends?

_____
_____
_____

What are practical ways that you can pursue justice in your community?

_____
_____
_____

What are practical ways that you can do what is just in your job?

_____
_____
_____

CHAPTER SIX:
WHAT DOES THE BIBLE SAY ABOUT SAME-SEX RELATIONSHIPS?

Written By Yana Jenay Conner

Introduction

I distinctly remember where I was when I learned that the Federal government legalized same-sex marriage. I was sitting at a local coffee shop's bar, procrastinating. I was supposed to be working on my seminary homework, but instead, I was scrolling through Facebook. To be honest, the ruling didn't shock me. What shocked me was the hashtag attached to the news.

#lovewins

Ouch! This hashtag felt like an indictment on the Church—a fair one, but it stung nonetheless, A LOT. Historically, Christians have treated the LGBTQ+ community with very little empathy, concern, or love. And with the passing of same-sex marriage, they were acting as what my grandma would refer to as a "plum fool" on the internet.

As I scrolled through social media, I read story after story of friends who, unbeknownst to me, identified as part of the LGBTQ+ community and had been deeply hurt by the Church. From being met with silence when they confided and shared their same-sex attraction to feeling like their only option was isolation and hiding after being met with harsh words from the pulpit, and many others. One theme carried through all of them—my friends were filled with pain.

Unable to hide my grief, I cried. I was overwhelmed with emotion for my friends who had been so deeply hurt. It saddens me to know that a whole community of people felt so unloved by the very people who are to be marked by love. I mean, Love is supposed to be what Chrsitians do, *right?*

The second greatest commandment, "love your neighbor as yourself (Matthew 22:39)."

Jesus' command to us was to love others as He has loved us (John 15:12)."

Jesus also makes it abundantly clear that loving others is what it means to be His disciple (John 13:35).

As Christians, we are to possess a winsome love.

Which leads me to ask: How do we extend biblical love to members of the LGBTQ+ community and affirm biblical convictions about **sexuality**?

In this chapter, we will discuss how we can extend biblical love to those in the LGBTQ+ community while affirming biblical convictions. We will also explore the various views taken within the church.

At the end of the lesson, you'll be able to answer the following questions:

1. What is the difference between the affirming and non-affirming views?

2. What are the two primary views of same-sex relationships?

3. What are the major arguments of the affirming view?

4. What are the major arguments of the non-affirming view?

5. What is the difference between same-sex attraction, same-sex relationships, and same-sex intercourse? Why is this nuanced language important to the discussion around sexuality and faith?

6. Between the affirming and non-affirming views, which one is most aligned with Scriptures teaching?

7. What does Andrew Marin's research reveal about the LGBTQ+ general disposition towards faith?

8. What are some practical ways you can extend biblical love to members of the LGBTQ+ community while also holding biblical convictions?

Glossary (In Order of Appearance

- **Same-Sex Relationship Affirming View:** The view that God affirms same-sex relationships and intercourse.

- **Same-Sex- Relationship Non-Affirming View:** The view that God does not affirm same-sex relationships and intercourse.

- **Paul's Sexual Ethic:** The conclusion that because Jesus never talked about homosexuality and the passages in the New Testament that condemn homosexuality were written by Paul that those views are Paul's opinions, not Christ's.

 A LOOK AT THE PAST

Within the Christian community, there are two primary views on same-sex relationships: *same-sex relationship affirming and same-sex relationship non-affirming*. However, before we discuss them, it's important to note that many people find their sexuality to be more complex than being attracted to or being in a relationship with someone of the same sex. These complexities explain why identifying categories within the LGBTQ+

community are not just lesbian and gay, but include bi-sexual, queer, questioning, asexual, and pansexual. Though many may feel this kind of nuance of sexuality is unnecessary or even pretentious, this diversity of categories reveals three things:

1. In the society we live in, accurately understanding and expressing one's sexuality is a supreme value.
2. For many, sexuality has become a primary way of understanding and constructing their identity.
3. Many people are deeply confused about their sexuality.

Regardless of personal views, it's important that Christians move towards those identifying as part of the LGBTQ+ community with empathy, listening, and nuance. In *God and the Gay Christian: A Biblical Case in Support of Same-Sex Relationships*, Matthew Vines, suggests moving away from labels such as "*conservative* and *liberal, evangelical* and *progressive,* and even *traditionalist* and *revisionist*" when discussing our stance on sexuality since "no label conveys the same meaning to every person."[44] Terms such as affirming and non-affirming are much clearer, more respectful, and less political.

Christians who hold to the same-sex relationship affirming viewpoint believe "committed, monogamous same-sex relationships" are not sinful. Christians who hold to the same-sex relationship non-affirming view believe marriage by God's design is between a man and a woman. It's important to note, the majority of those who hold to the same-sex relationship affirming view do not affirm the authority of Scripture impacts their interpretation of Old and New Testament passages on homosexuality.

In Old Testament passages, such as Genesis 19:5, Leviticus 18:22, Leviticus 20:13 that condemn same-sex relationships, those who hold to the same-sex affirming view conclude that because these verses are under the Old Covenant, they have no bearing on those who live under the New Covenant.

In regards to New Testament passages that condemn same-sex

---

44. Matthew Vines, God and the Gay Christian: A Biblical Case For Same-Sex Relationships (New York, NY: Crown Publishing Group, 2014), 25.

relationships, such as Romans 1:26-27, 1 Corinthians 6:9-10, and 1 Timothy 1:9-10, they conclude that these texts are **Paul's sexual ethic**, not Jesus'. The suggest that Jesus nor any of the other New Testament writers condemns same-sex relationships except Paul. So, they chalk it up to those New Testament passages as Paul going rogue and creating a sexual ethic that is incongruent with the teaching of Christ that centers on love.

Though the majority of Christians who hold to the same-sex relationship affirming view do not affirm the authority of Scripture, there is a small minority within this group that affirm both same-sex relationships and the authority of Scripture. Among them is Matthew Vines, who argues for a "biblical case in support of same-sex relationships" in light of the psychological impact of the same-sex relationship non-affirming view and a cultural-historical understanding of sexuality in ancient times.

Psychological Impact

One of Vines' cornerstone arguments in favor of the same-sex relationship affirming view is based on the "destructive (psychological) consequences brought on by the non-affirming view. He writes, "Sadly, negative attitudes toward gay relationships have led to crippling depression, torment, suicide, and alienation from God and the church."[45] Because these consequences are "contrary to God's nature" and not congruent with the fruit God desires in our lives, Vines suggests the church ask itself: "Do the destructive consequences of long-held views among Christians warrant a reinterpretation of Scripture?"[46] He grounds this question in Jesus' teaching that bad trees bear bad fruit. He argues that because the same-sex relationship non-affirming view bears bad fruit, depression, shame, and suicide, the tree (being its teaching) must also be bad and contrary to what Jesus wants for those created in His image.

---

45. Ibid, 25.
46. Ibid., 24.

Cultural-Historical Understanding of Sexuality

The other crux of Vines' argument for the same-sex relationship affirming view relates to the way sexuality was viewed and understood during ancient times. With references to the writings of ancient philosophers, like Plato, Zeno, and Musonius Rufus, Vines points out that "for the majority of human history, homosexuality was not seen as a different sexual orientation that distinguished a minority of people from the heterosexual majority. Instead, it was a manifestation of normal sexual desire pursued (in) excess." Given this historical understanding of the Roman-Greco ancient world, Vines concludes that Scripture's condemnation of same-sex relationships was not "committed, monogamous same-sex relationships," but rather their insatiable sexual appetites.

For this reason, when interpreting Old Testament passages, such as Genesis 19:5, Vines and others who share his view believe Sodom and Gomorrah were not condemned because men were having sex with men, but because men were having sex with men in excess. This understanding also carries over to his interpretation of New Testament passages, such as Romans 1:26-27, which based on Paul's reference to idolatry, Vine believes Paul is condemning their excessive pursuit of same-sex intercourse apart from a committed, monogamous relationship. In his view, what Paul is claiming to be "unnatural" is their same-sex promiscuity that is fueled by lust and not love.

Though Vines and other scholars present more arguments for their views taken from Scripture, history, and personal experience, the goal of this chapter is to present the general and most unique arguments for the same-sex relationships affirming view.

REFLECTION QUESTIONS:

In 2-3 words, describe how conversations about sexuality and Christianity make you feel?

_____

_____

_____

What do you believe are the best arguments for the affirming view? What are its flaws?

_____

_____

_____

WHAT DOES THE BIBLE SAY?

In light of our presupposition that the Bible is inerrant, infallible, and authoritative, our belief is that the most aligned view with Scripture is same-sex relationship non-affirming view. Even those who hold to the affirming view agree the non-affirming view is the most logical view for those who affirm the Scripture's authority. They just don't agree or accept it.

There are six passages in Scripture that have served as the "battlegrounds" for this discussion. Three in the Old Testament and three in the New. colleagues who hold to the affirming view have a good argument in suggesting that the (Old Testament) commands in Leviticus 18:22 and Leviticus 20:13 were under the Old Covenant and have no bearing on how we live under the New Covenant that came through Jesus Christ. However, what are we to do with the story of the destruction of Sodom and Gomorrah in Genesis 19:1-29, which was given prior to the law? (If you're not familiar with it, this is a good place to stop and read it.)

In Genesis 18:16-33, God revealed to Abraham that He would

destroy the town because of its inhabitants' extreme sin. Many conclude extreme sin refers to same-sex intercourse. However, like those of the affirming view have pointed out, God did not reveal the nature of Sodom and Gomorrah's sin and therefore it's unfair to assume homosexual sex is what led to its destruction. Vines would add that it was the excessive of their sin that God sought to condemn, not homosexuality in general. Though these points are valid, it seems as though the author of Genesis, Moses, who was inspired by God to tell the story, is seeking to teach us something about God's view on sex and sexuality.

We have a clearer picture of God's view on sex and sexuality in passages such as Leviticus 18:22 and Leviticus 20:13. In these two verses, God commands the Israelites to "not sleep with a man as with a woman" (Leviticus 18:22). Here are two observations to consider in light of Vines' argument:

These two passages do not make a distinction between same-sex intercourse in excess or in a committed relationship. They only speak to the act itself.

Though Vines' is accurate in stating that same-sex intercourse was a norm in the Greco-Roman world. It is important to remember the laws in Leviticus were given to the people of Israel by God, to set them apart from the other nations around them. They were to live in harmony with God's commands, not the norms of the world around them.

To be fair, those who affirm same-sex relationships present a very thoughtful and reasonable interpretation of Old Testament passages. Especially when suggesting that Old Testament commands no longer hold given that we are under the New Covenant that has come through Jesus Christ, fulfilling the law. Though this is an excellent observation, there were two kinds of commands in Leviticus: *ritual laws* and *moral commands*. This leads us to ask, is the Old Testament's objection to same-sex relationships a ritual law or a moral command?

Given that the Old Testament's objections to same-sex relationships carry over to the teaching of the New Testament, it appears the objection to same-sex relationships is a moral command. In the verses below, they are mentioned alongside other moral commands that found their start in the Old Testament and are still objected to in the New Testament. Take a look.

Romans 1:26-27
"For this reason God delivered them over to disgraceful passions. Their women exchanged natural sexual relations for unnatural ones. The men in the same way also left natural relations with women and were inflamed in their lust for one another. Men committed shameless acts with men and received in their own persons the appropriate penalty of their error."

1 Corinthians 6:9-10
"Do not be deceived: No sexually immoral people, idolaters, adulterers, or males who have sex with males, no thieves, greedy people, drunkards, verbally abusive people, or swindlers will inherit God's kingdom."

1 Timothy 1:9-10
"We know that the law is not meant for a righteous person, but for the lawless and rebellious, for the ungodly and sinful, for the unholy and irrelevant, for those who kill their fathers and mothers, for murderers, for the sexually immoral and males who have sex with males, for slave traders, liars, perjurers, and for whatever else is contrary to the sound teaching."

As previously stated, those who do not affirm the Bible as authoritative refer to these passages as Paul's Sexual Ethic. However, for those of us who believe the Bible is the inspired word of God, we receive these words as God's words, not Paul's.

Additionally, we must remember how the books and letters in the Bible came to be recognized as the inspired Word of God, meaning the Early Church recognized Paul's letters as authoritative and trustworthy in life and doctrine. Even Peter, who walked closely with Jesus, recognized Paul's words as Scripture (2 Peter 3:15-16). If anyone would know Jesus' thoughts on sexuality, it would be Peter.

That being said, I want to draw your attention to Peter's words that "some of Paul's teachings are hard to understand." Though we can't fully know what Peter is referring to, I imagine we can identify with his feelings. The Bible's teaching about same-sex relationships is tough. Especially for those who are same-sex attracted. While the Bible says same-sex intercourse is unnatural, their same-sex attraction feels very natural. They cannot envision themselves being in a romantic relationship with a person of the opposite sex. So the Bible's teaching is incredibly heavy and confusing for them. To accept and live by the Bible's teaching could mean a life of celibacy, a life in which they will have to reimagine family.

This is why empathy, listening, and compassion are so critical for the Church when it comes to engaging with those of the LGBTQ+ community. Don't bulldoze over people's feelings in the name of Biblical convictions. This is neither loving nor God-honoring.

REFLECTION QUESTIONS:

How does the Bible's teaching on same-sex intercourse impact you?

_____

_____

_____

_____

Of the affirming and non-affirming views, which one do you find most compelling? Why?

_____

_____

_____

_____

IS RECONCILATION POSSIBLE?

I don't have to tell you how hurtful the dialogue between the Church and the LGBTQ+ community has been. Both parties feel hurt, misunderstood, unloved, and unsure of how to move towards one another. When we look at that divide, it's hard to think reconciliation is possible.

However, in his book, *Us Versus Us: The Untold Story of Religion and the LGBT Community*, Andrew Marin shares research that proves the Church and the LGBTQ+ community have more in common than one would think. Here are some of his most surprising findings:

- 86% of LGBTQ+ were raised in a faith community from 0-18[47]
- 54% of LGBTQ+ people leave their religious community after the age of 18[48]
- 76% of LGBTQ+ people are open to returning to their religious community and its practices[49]
- 80% of LGBTQ+ people regularly pray regardless of religious identification or affiliation.[50]

Take those numbers in for a moment.

More than 3/4 of the LGBTQ+ were raised in a faith community. In his research, Marin defined "raised in a faith community" as participating in a church service or activity twice a week. Of the 54% that leave their religious community after the age of 18, the overwhelming majority left because they didn't feel safe or were kicked out.[51] Only a small minority left because of their church's theological stances on same-sex relationships. Some even reported that the unwillingness of the church to talk about sexuality led to their departure.

Can you imagine the rejection? The confusion and heartache of not having someone in your faith community willing to talk or

---

47. Andrew Marin, Us Versus Us: The Untold Story of Religion and the LGBT community (Colorado Springs, CO: NavPress, 2016), 1.
48. Ibid, 31.
49. Ibid, 65.
50. Ibid, 113.
51. Ibid, 37.

help you sift through your questions about sexuality? Can you feel the pain of being "kicked out" of a community that raised you? A community where everyone knows your name? A community with whom you have celebrated birthdays, graduations, and just about every childhood milestone? Can you imagine the abandonment? The hurt?

However, when asked, "Would you be open to returning to your community of faith and its practices?," 76% of the LGBTQ+ said yes.[52] This high percentage reveals that many within the LGBTQ+ community have a sincere desire to be connected to God and a community of faith. Here are six factors those who are open to returning said would influence their decision to return:

- Feeling Loved (12%)
- Given Time (9%)
- Faith Community's Change in Theology (8%)
- No Attempts to Change Their Sexual Orientation (6%)
- Authenticity (5%)
- Support of Family and Friends (4%)

The data shows that there is so much opportunity when it comes to engaging and reconciling with those in the LGBTQ+ community. The Church can easily deliver five out of six of these factors.

 WHAT DOES THIS MEAN FOR APOLOGETICS?

Here are five practical ways you can make it a both/and instead of an either/or when extending biblical love to the LGBTQ+ community while also holding to biblical convictions about sexuality.

Ask Questions, Don't Assume

Marin's research reveals that there is so much Christians misunderstand about the LGBTQ+ community. As a whole, they have been characterized as a community that is hostile to conversations about faith and wants nothing to do with the church. Though that may be true to some, the numbers tell us that far more would not only be open to a conversation about faith but

---
52. Ibid, 65.

would likely even welcome it. We need to move past our assumptions, ask questions, and not allow the rhetoric in the media to paralyze us from talking to people in the LGBTQ+ community about their spiritual background, faith, and their sexuality.

Dialogues over Debates

Due to the hurt caused by the Church, we need to enter into conversations with the LGBTQIA+ community with a sincere heart to listen and learn, not debate. In other words, don't pick a fight or feel the need to object when you disagree. They know you don't agree! But what they don't know is that your love is unconditional. Love that requires agreement as a prerequisite is not biblical love. God loved us before we brought our lives into agreement with Him. He sent His Son to die for the sins of the whole world, knowing that many would not agree with Him. Agreement was not a prerequisite for Him and it shouldn't be for us.

> **Love that requires agreement as a prerequisite is not biblical love.**

People Are People, Not Projects

Often, when we intentionally build relationships for the sake of sharing the gospel, they can easily become projects, instead of human beings who need to be known and loved. We view them as sinners who need to be fixed or as a goal that needs to be accomplished. Build authentic relationships and check task-oriented behaviors at the door. Prioritize the relationship over "producing fruit" or "watering seeds."

Seeing them as a whole person, not just their sexuality sets the foundation for an authentic relationship. Let them help you. Let them teach you. Let them give you advice on things you're not good at. This posture helps remove the "savior mentality" that many Christians can project when they are in relationships with people who are unbelievers and make the relationship mutual.

Be a Safe Place

From Marin's research, we learn that love and support would encourage a return to faith. Both of those qualities lead to a feeling of safety. And given that most of them left the Church because they didn't feel safe, this is a good show of faith as to where to start.

Safety comes from the assurance that we will love them and not leave them relationally when we disagree or they don't meet our expectations. We also help people feel safe when we listen, don't interrupt, and ask thoughtful questions that show our eagerness to understand their point of view. We can specifically make those in the LGBTQ+ community feel safe when we give them a safe place to process their sexuality and their faith, allowing them to express their confusion, anger, sadness, desires, etc.

Great Commission AND Great Commandment

The Great Commission and the Great Commandment should never be in competition with one another. Instead, they should work in concert. We are called to make disciples, but this command is not to undermine Christ's command to love our neighbor as ourselves. Neither should loving our neighbor as ourselves undermine the call to make disciples. At times, it will be hard to discern when to speak up and when to be quiet or when to confront and when to let go. But we need to live within this tension of both/and in order to extend biblical love to those in the LGBTQ+ community while holding to our biblical convictions.

REFLECTION QUESTIONS:

What did the statistics about the LGBTQ+ community and the results of the study reveal to you? How did they confront or challenge your biases?

_____

_____

_____

_____

In light of factors that would cause those in the LBGTQ+ community to be open to returning to their communities of faith, what would you add to the list of practical ways the church can move forward in love and conviction?

_____

_____

_____

_____

COURAGEOUS CONVERSATIONS

THE ONLINE COURSE

Take course at learn.jude3project.org. For 15% off, use promo code: book

SMALL GROUP CURRICULUMS

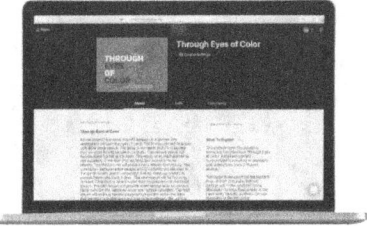
ONLINE COURSES

JUDE 3 MERCH

Available at jude3project.org or use the QR code below:

BECOME A MONTHLY FINANCIAL PARTNER
EVERY GIFT HELPS EQUIP

JUDE3PROJECT.ORG/DONATE

www.ingramcontent.com/pod-product-compliance
Lightning Source LLC
Chambersburg PA
CBHW071252070526
44583CB00017B/2443